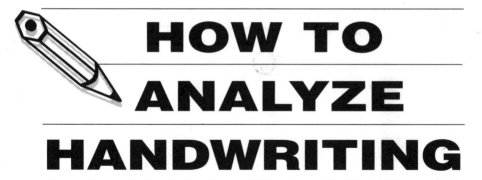

HOW TO ANALYZE HANDWRITING

to reveal the innermost secrets of personality!

Reviewed and endorsed by Victoria Mertes,
Master Handwriting Expert, Beverly Hills, California

By Alison Bell

Illustrated by Jack White

RANDOM HOUSE   NEW YORK

To my wonderfully supportive father

—*A. B.*

Library of Congress Cataloging-in-Publication Data:

Bell, Alison.
How to analyze handwriting to reveal the innermost secrets of personality! / by Alison
Bell; illustrated by Jack White : reviewed and endorsed by Victoria Mertes.
    p.   cm.—(Kidbacks)
ISBN 0-679-87089-X (pbk.)
1. Graphology—Juvenile literature. [1. Graphology.]
I. White, Jack, ill. II. Title. III. Series.
BF891.B45 1994
155.2'82—dc20   94-41589

Manufactured in the United States of America   10 9 8 7 6 5 4 3 2 1

contents

Hi! You don't know me, but after you read this book, you'll be able to tell a lot about me just by studying my handwriting. I know it sounds hard to believe, but it's true!

Alison Ball

That's right. By looking at these few sentences, you'll be able to tell if I'm outgoing or shy, happy or sad, organized or messy, nervous or calm. Handwriting reflects people's personalities. It reveals how people are feeling, what their strong points are, their weaknesses, their likes and dislikes, and much more!

The study of handwriting, also called graphology, is an informative, fascinating *science*. Graphologists, also called handwriting analysts or graphoanalysts, believe that people's handwritings tell as much about them as their actions or words.

Why does handwriting reveal so much about all of us? Because every time you put pen or pencil to paper, your hand isn't doing the writing, your *brain* is. Your brain decides how you dot your "i's," how big you write, and whether you slant your words to the left or to the right—

without you even thinking about it. Your handwriting, or "brain writing," as some graphologists believe handwriting should be called, is a direct expression of the inner you.

Because everyone thinks differently, no two people's handwriting looks exactly the same. In fact, you are so programmed to write a certain way that you would *still* have the same handwriting if you were suddenly forced to write holding a pen in your mouth or between your toes. Studies of thousands of people who have lost the use of their hands and have had to learn to write with their mouth or toes show that they eventually produce the same handwriting they did when they used their hands!

Once small children learn how to write cursive—that is, in script—they will work on this skill a few years before their handwriting begins looking consistent. Usually by the time they reach nine or ten, kids write the same way almost every time they put pen or pencil to paper.

Look back over some of your handwritten letters or notes from the past year—you'll be surprised by how constant your writing style is!

However, this isn't to say that a person's handwriting *never* changes. Everyone's handwriting fluctuates slightly every now and then. When people are sick, their handwriting usually becomes fainter because they don't press down on the pen or pencil with the usual energy. Moods can also affect how people write (this will be explained more in the following chapters). Time is a factor, too. The more rushed a person is, the more sloppy and illegible his or her handwriting will be. But if someone always has sloppy handwriting, the writer may have at least some trouble relating his or her thoughts and feelings to others.

Sometimes people with sloppy cursive writing will print instead because they feel that's the only way their writing can be understood. (By the way, graphologists believe that sometimes people print instead of writing in script because they're trying to cover up who they are. They're scared that their handwriting will reveal too much about them.) Others may throw in a printed word now and then just to be creative or different.

Despite these occasional changes, graphologists believe that people's handwriting is "fixed" enough for an analyst to look at almost any handwriting sample and get an accurate personality profile of the person who wrote it.

In this book, you'll learn how to use handwriting analysis to gain insight into your own personality as well as those of your friends, family, and anyone else you want to know more about—including your favorite celebrity! Each chapter in the book will teach you how to analyze one element of a person's handwriting, such as a signature or how the person writes the pronoun "I." At the end of each chapter are exercises for you to practice your newfound graphology skills on friends, family, and even yourself.

Before long, you'll be able to look at anything handwritten—a letter, a grocery list, a note passed to you in class—and figure out what makes its writer tick. You'll also have a hobby "at your fingertips" that will entertain and enlighten you for the rest of your life!

Choose Your Writing Weapon

Graphologists believe that the type of writing tool people choose also tells a lot about their personalities.

If you prefer to write with a pencil: You're probably a tad hesitant about putting forth your ideas and beliefs. You're the type who often says to yourself, "Gee, I wish I hadn't said that!" or "How could I have done that?"—even if you haven't said or done anything wrong. The desire to "erase" what you say and do in life is reflected by writing with a pencil—you always have the option of erasing what you just wrote!

Of course, preferring to write with a pencil when you're taking a test doesn't count. Obviously you'll want to use a pencil because there's the likelihood you'll need to go back and revise an answer.

If you prefer to write with a felt-tipped pen: You probably like to be noticed. You want everyone to know who you are and all the great things you have to offer. By the way, what color ink you choose can be revealing as well. For example, if you choose to write with a hot pink or purple pen, you're probably (and fairly obviously) a lot more flamboyant than a person who writes with black ink!

If you prefer to write with a fine-tipped ballpoint pen: You like to be in charge and get things done. The ballpoint pen gives you smooth control over your writing — plus it's fast and accurate.

chapter 7

the history of graphology

People have been fascinated by the study of handwriting for hundreds of years. Many influential people throughout history—such as the writers John Keats, Edgar Allan Poe, Robert Browning, Sir Walter Scott, Johann Wolfgang von Goethe, Anton Chekhov, and the physicist Albert Einstein—have noticed that there is a link between handwriting and personality. For example, Sir Walter Scott, a Scottish writer who lived from 1771 to 1832, wrote in 1827 in his novel *Chronicles of the Canongate*, "I could not help thinking, according to an opinion I have heard seriously maintained, that something of a man's character may be conjectured from his handwriting."

One of the first people to show an interest in handwriting analysis was an eleventh-century Chinese painter and philosopher named Kuo Jo Hsu. Kuo noted, "Handwriting can infallibly show whether it comes from a person who is noble-minded, or from one who is vulgar."

It took another five hundred years, however, for the first study of handwriting to be recorded on paper. In 1624, an Italian professor of philosophy named Camillo Baldi wrote *Trattato*, which was a "treatise" on handwriting. Baldi's work was basically ignored by everyone—except for some traveling magicians who learned his technique and used it to entertain rich noblemen. Baldi's findings are amazingly accurate when compared to modern graphology. He believed that handwriting revealed a lot about a person's intelligence and physical health, just as today's graphologists maintain.

Then, around 1840, a group of French churchmen working in a hospital noticed that the handwriting of sick patients was different from that of healthy people. One of these men, the Abbé Jean-Hippolyte Michon, became very interested in the study of handwriting and spent the next thirty years collecting and studying writing samples. He isolated different strokes used in handwriting and assigned personality traits to each of them. It was he who coined the word "graphology" (from the Greek words *gráphein,* to write, and *-ology,* science). Michon went on to found the Society of Graphology in Paris in 1871 and to publish two major works on graphology in 1872 and 1877, both of which generated a lot of enthusiasm for the subject throughout Europe.

In the early 1900s, a German philosopher named Ludwig Klages wrote five books on handwriting analysis, becoming the leading expert in graphology. He was the first to study a handwriting sample as a whole, instead of as a collection of individual strokes.

Today graphology is a respected science in the United States, as well as in France, Germany, Switzerland, Austria, and Israel. Some colleges, such as the University of California at Los Angeles, even teach courses in it. Other colleges incorporate handwriting analysis into psychology classes. Several independent graphological societies, such as the

Tools of the Trade

Professional graphologists depend on the following equipment to accurately analyze handwriting samples:

➡ a magnifying glass to see the strokes better

➡ a ruler to measure the baseline

➡ a protractor to measure the slant

As you begin analyzing friends' and family members' handwriting, grab these tools to help you.

National Society for Graphology, located in New York City, teach courses and award top students certificates in professional graphology. Another well-known society is the American Association of Handwriting Analysts in Downers Grove, Illinois, just outside Chicago.

Professional graphology is a fast-growing field. Businesses around the country, such as a jewelry manufacturing firm, a jewelry distributor, and a trucking company (all of which have asked to remain anonymous), have begun employing graphologists on a part-time basis to determine if potential employees are hardworking, reliable, and honest, or if certain employees should be promoted or not. Some colleges call upon graphologists to help them decide which students to accept. And psychologists regularly hire graphologists to help them learn more about their patients.

But the biggest (and most exciting) field of work for professional graphologists is in crime solving. Police departments around the world, including the FBI and Scotland Yard, regularly employ graphologists to analyze handwriting samples of people suspected of committing crimes to find out if they have the personalities of criminals.

Police also hire graphologists to study handwritten hate notes and death threats sent to political leaders, celebrities, and other potential victims of crimes. The graphologists can often determine which writers are most likely to try to act on their threats.

Graphologists predict that in the years to come their services will be used even more widely. So don't be too surprised if in five years, when applying for a job at a fast-food franchise, you're asked to submit a handwriting sample in order to determine your ability to flip burgers!

Case Closed!

Andrea McNichol is a professional graphologist who has been consulted by law enforcement agencies across the country. The following is one of her cases, as related in her book, *Handwriting Analysis: Putting It to Work for You.*

One day McNichol got a call from a private security firm representing the owner of a large medical office. Someone had been repeatedly setting fires in a plastic surgeon's office on the seventh floor of the building. There were many possible suspects because the plastic surgeon had a lot of enemies among his patients and staff. Could McNichol inspect the handwriting samples of the suspects and determine if any of them had the angry, unstable personality of an arsonist?

She agreed to take the case. There was one problem with it, however. The security firm that had hired the graphologist was under strict orders to keep the investigation secret, so McNichol couldn't simply *ask* every suspect for a handwriting sample. Instead, she had to sneak into the office at night wearing a cleaning woman's uniform and search through desks and wastepaper baskets for the needed samples (all the time hoping that the suspected arsonist would not enter the office and catch her rifling his or her garbage).

Almost immediately, McNichol noticed that one of the samples she'd found was full of abnormal letter shapes and words with the letters pushed closely together—signs of anger and instability in writing. McNichol quickly called the firm and told them she had a suspect!

The security firm put the person under surveillance. And some weeks later, sure enough, the suspect was discovered entering the building with a fire-making device concealed in a briefcase. Due to McNichol's handwriting-sample sleuthing, the case was closed!

lean and mean:
the slant of handwriting

When graphologists talk about the slant of handwriting, they mean the direction in which it leans. A person's handwriting either leans to the left, leans to the right, goes straight up and down, or leans in all different directions.

Graphologists believe that the slant of handwriting tells how outgoing a person is. In general, the more a person's handwriting slants to the right, the more social he or she is.

The slant also reveals how a person feels about the past and the future. Handwriting analysts view the left side of a piece of paper as the past and the right-hand side as the future because we write from left to right, which makes the first words in a line "older" than the last words written. Therefore, graphologists believe that if your handwriting slants to the left, you prefer spending time alone and thinking about past events, and if your handwriting slants to the right, you are interested in meeting and being with new people, as well as planning for the future.

The Different Types of Slants

When studying a person's slant, look for the way his or her handwriting *most often* leans. This will most accurately suggest the writer's personality traits.

Slanting to the Right

lean to the right

If your handwriting slants to the right, you're probably a friendly, open person. Think of words slanted to the right as a person leaning forward as he or she talks to a friend. You're the type of person who, when you spot a new kid sitting alone in the cafeteria, will invite him or her to join your friends. You most likely have a lot of friends—and can't wait to make even more!

You're probably very tuned in to the future. You can't wait to go to college, get a job, or start having adventures.

Slanting to the Left

lean to the left

If you write this way, you're probably a private person. You don't feel comfortable sharing your feelings with a person until you know that person well. It's not that you're unfriendly, you just need a little more time to warm up to people.

You're also no doubt very attached to the past. No one will ever stand between you and your best pal from kindergarten—even if you rarely speak to him or her now! Once you make a friend and share a history with him or her, that person is a buddy for life.

Writing Straight Up and Down

straight up and down

If you most often write vertically, you probably enjoy being in control. You're cool, calm, and collected. You're neither too attached to the past or overly wrapped up in daydreaming about the future. You prefer to live day to day, making the most of each moment.

Writing in Different Directions

every which way

If your writing typically switches directions within one sample, chances are you love change and have dozens of interests to prove it, from rock-climbing to Pog collecting to playing the harmonica.

You may also be a bit on the moody side. One day you say "hi" to everyone at school, the next day you don't even feel like talking to your best friend.

Or you may simply write every which way because you're feeling confused about the whole idea of growing up. On one hand, you're tired of being a kid; on the other, you're scared stiff of getting older, gaining more responsibility, and dealing with dilemmas, like how to survive a blind date. The different slants reflect this confusion.

Another reason you may slant your writing to the right and left may simply be your age. Many young people write with different slants because their hand muscles aren't fully developed yet. When teens reach anywhere from thirteen to fifteen years, their writing usually begins to slant consistently in one direction.

How Mood Affects Handwriting Slant

While people write with one type of slant most of the time, sometimes their slant can change depending on how they're feeling at a particular moment. For instance, if you're feeling in a super-social mood at a party, your handwriting might slant far to the right. If, however, you're in a quiet mood and wish you were home watching TV, your handwriting might slant more to the left.

14

When One Word or Phrase Is Slanted Differently

Sometimes people give away their feelings about someone or something by the way they slant a certain word. When one word or phrase is slanted differently from the others in a sentence, you can bet that means something!

In general, graphologists believe that if, when you're writing, you lean a word or phrase to the right, you feel positive about it. If you write a word or phrase straight up and down or lean it to the left, you probably feel neutral or negative about it.

Look at this sentence. Which words are slanted differently?

I'm completely in love with my tennis teacher!

The words "in love" lean much more to the right. What does that say about the writer? He or she is really crazy about that instructor! In fact, the writer is so carried away by his or her strong emotions, the words look as if they could almost carry themselves off the page!

Next, look at this sentence.

I'm really excited about your party.

Notice how the word "excited" is up and down while the rest of the sentence leans to the right. The writer pulls back when he reaches this word. What do you think this says about how he *really* feels about the party? It may mean something like this:

"Your party will probably be a big yawn, but at least there'll be some good food there, and I won't have to spend the night at home listening to my sister practice the viola."

Or how about this sentence:

My parents said I have to stay home. Bummer!

The word "parents" slants to the left. This reflects how the writer feels toward her parents right now: frustrated!

Write On! Exercise #1

To see how your moods influence your handwriting, chart your handwriting for the next week. Every day at the same time, write down the sentence "I wonder if my slant has changed today." Next to the sentence, write down how you're feeling at that moment—happy, sad, frustrated, excited. After a week, look back over your handwriting and compare each slant with the mood you were in when you were writing. How much did your mood affect your slant?

Do the "Right" Thing

Most people slant their words to the right because that is the way they were taught to do in school. Why? Because we write from left to right across the page. When your hand is moving from left to right, it's natural to also slant your handwriting to the right.

And why is most of the world's population, except for those in the Middle East and parts of Asia, taught to write from left to right? Well, if you're right-handed (and almost nine out of ten people are), you're less likely to smear the words writing from left to right, than from right to left.

If you're right-handed, try writing with a pen from right to left on a piece of paper. After just one sentence, your hand is an inky mess!

The Slant Chart

Graphologists use the following chart to more exactly pin-point what the slant of people's handwriting says about how outgoing they are. Here, the degrees of slants have been labeled by letter, but some graphologists attach a number to each different slant.

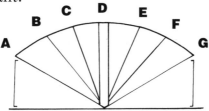

An "A" slant:

You're a very private person who shuns being in the spotlight.

A "B" slant: *hello*

You sometimes come off as a little cold, but you're actually just a bit on the shy side. Once people get to know you, you really open up.

A "C" slant: *hello*

You're a little reserved and cautious when it comes to making new friends, but in general you enjoy getting to know new people.

A "D" slant: *hello*

While you like the company of other people, you aren't dependent on them to make you happy. You're just as content when left alone to think.

An "E" slant: *hello*

You're friendly and open, even though you don't reveal everything about yourself. You crave a few hours of time alone now and then.

An "F" slant: *hello*

You love people and love to open up about yourself. Sometimes, however, you may feel you've told too much, such as the time you revealed your secret admiration for your math teacher to your brother—and he blabbed it all over school!

A "G" slant: *hello*

You're such a complete people person that it's hard for you to handle any time alone. Why be by yourself when you have so many friends you can be with?

Write On! Exercise #2

Write "hello" on a blank piece of paper and try to determine where *you* fit in on the slant chart. Not only does the slant of your writing reveal how social you are, it also tells how you feel about the future. The farther your handwriting slants to the right, the more forward-looking a person you are. The farther it leans to the left, the more attached to the past you are. Are you surprised by how much your slant reveals about you?

sizing up the situation: the size of handwriting

Some people write so large that they fill an entire page with only a few sentences. Other people's writing is so tiny they can fit ten paragraphs onto a small thank-you card.

When graphologists study the size of a person's handwriting, they think of the blank piece of paper as the writer's world—his or her family, friends, school, activities, and so on. How big a person writes on the page tells whether a person tends to reach out to or pull back from the people and events surrounding him or her. It also reveals how someone approaches life—in an enthusiastic "big" way or with a more subdued, "smaller" attitude.

Large Handwriting

I have confidence.

In general, people who write with large handwriting are very outgoing, confident, and excited about life. They're probably involved in a million projects. Just as their handwriting fills up the page, they like to fill their lives with different people and hobbies. Not surprisingly, many actors and politicians have large handwriting.

If your handwriting is large, it might mean:

☞ You want to be seen as big and important. Your writing says "Hey, look at me!"

☞ You're not super-detail-oriented. Instead, you see the big picture in life. For example, you love to come up with grand schemes, such as starting a school magazine. You're great at coming up with a name for the magazine and persuading all of your friends to write articles. But when it comes to the nitty-gritty—writing, editing, printing, and distributing the magazine—you're not interested. Someone else can do *that*, thank you very much!

☞ You crave space in life. You hate to be told what to do (especially by parental units) and feel confined easily. Your idea of school heaven is taking all of your classes outside.

☞ You do things in a big way. Like the time you planned your best friend's surprise birthday party and persuaded your parents to turn their house into a dance club, complete with a performance by the local grunge band!

Average-Size Writing

I'm just your average Joe Writer.

If your handwriting is about this size, you're probably very well balanced. You juggle your friends and hobbies without, for the most part, feeling overwhelmed. You're comfortable with yourself and don't feel the need to prove anything to anyone.

Small Handwriting

I like details!

If you are a P.W.S.H. (Person with Small Handwriting), you are probably very detail-oriented and disciplined. In general, you're also less outgoing than people with big handwriting. A high percentage of scientists and mathematicians have small handwriting.

People who write this way usually like to follow the rules —i.e. they're not likely to talk back to a teacher, even if everyone else they know can't help but smart off to the old crab!

If you have small handwriting, it may mean:

☞ You have the concentration of ten algebra teachers! When you focus in on a project, nothing distracts you. As your mind narrows its focus, your handwriting does the same.

☞ You're a loner. You prefer to be alone or with a small group of friends.

☞ You feel small about yourself. You aren't as confident about yourself and your talents as you should be!

Super-Small Writing

You thought you'd seen everything, huh? Can you even read this?

Have you ever had a friend write to you whose writing was so small you almost had to whip out a magnifying glass to read it? People who write this small are often on the shy side. They "shrink" from other people, just the way their handwriting shrinks on the page. They're also very focused on themselves and their activities. If you write this way, you're probably the type who can do your math homework and listen to an Aerosmith album at the same time. Your powers of concentration are amazing!

22

Writing That Gets Larger

I love the sweater and will wear it often.

If your writing has a tendency to get bigger and bigger as you go along, it may be a sign that you're tired. The more tired you get, the less you concentrate and the bigger you write. Or you may simply be eager to finish whatever it is you're writing—such as a thank-you card to your aunt Ethel for the purple Barney sweater she knitted you for your *thirteenth* birthday!

Writing That Gets Smaller

The best shows on TV are on cable. Why, where would we be today without MTV?

The smaller your handwriting gets, generally speaking, the more interested you are in the subject matter at hand. For example, let's say your English teacher asks you to write an essay on what at first sounds like a boring topic: "Television: The Medium and Its Message." You're bummed until you realize that this is the perfect opportunity to vent your love/hate relationship with the characters on *Melrose Place*. Once you start writing, you become so engrossed in the essay you feel you could write for pages and pages. Your handwriting will reflect your growing interest by getting smaller and smaller.

When Certain Words Are Bigger Than Others

n general, if you write one word bigger than the others around it, you're showing that you think more of it. For example, notice which name is biggest in the following sentence:

Michael, **Adam**, Clay, and I went to the movies.

This writer is revealing that he likes Adam more than his other two pals. An overly large word may also show the depth of a person's feeling.

See the examples below:

I am so **embarrassed** about what I said.

This writer is really embarrassed about something.

This class is so boring.

This writer is bored out of his skull.

We're going **Skiing** this weekend!

This writer can't wait to hit the slopes.

Write On! Exercise #3

Do you have your eye on a gorgeous someone? By examining that person's handwriting size and comparing it with your own, you can see just how compatible you'd be if you ended up a couple.

Start by getting a handwriting sample of that special guy or girl. Next, determine if he or she writes with large, average, small, or super-small writing. Then look at your own handwriting to determine how large you write.

If you have the same size handwriting, you're probably a lot alike and will hit it off well (unless, of course, you both write with super-small handwriting and are too shy to make the first move!). If your sizes are different, the old saying "Opposites attract" may apply. For example, let's say you're attracted to someone with large handwriting, while yours is very tiny. You two may be a good match because he or she can help bring you out of your shyness shell, while you can help him or her get better at paying attention to the little details in life!

the straight scoop: baselines

When you write on an unlined piece of paper, your writing naturally either goes straight across, up or down, or else alternates between going up and going down. This unseen line your handwriting follows is what graphologists call a baseline. Even when they use lined paper, some people's handwriting will rise above or drop below the lines.

By looking at the baseline, graphologists can tell a person's attitude about the past, present, and future, as well as how motivated a person is to work on new projects and activities.

People's moods can also temporarily affect their baselines. People have a tendency to write on an upward slope when they're in a good mood and on a downward slope when they're in a bad mood.

A Baseline That Goes Up

I know I'll make the soccer team.

If you write uphill most of the time, it probably means you're "up" on life and not afraid to reach for your goals. You're also a bit of a dreamer and love to "reach for the stars."

A Baseline That Goes Down

I hope I'll make the soccer team.

If you write downhill naturally, it may be just because of your age. Many children write downhill because they are still developing their hand muscles and it's easier to write downhill than uphill.

If an adult or teenager writes this way consistently, it may mean that the writer is as down on life as his or her handwriting. The person may also be scared or insecure about what the future holds.

A Straight Baseline

I'll work very hard to make the soccer team.

If you write like this, you're on a straight and even course through life. You know what you want in life and work hard to get it, despite the odds.

A Baseline That Is Both Up and Down

Do you think I can make the soccer team?

If your baseline often shifts from up to down within one writing sample, it's a sign that you're constantly changing. One minute you're up, the next minute you're feeling down. One day you want to be a nurse practitioner, the next, a potter. Most likely, you're also very flexible and able to go with the flow.

A Baseline That Goes Up, Then Down

Maybe I won't go out for the dawn team after all.

If your baseline starts up and gradually works its way downward, you may have a hard time finishing things you start. You start a task with a lot of enthusiasm ("This weekend I'm going to organize my room, down to every last mismatched sock!"), then lose steam ("Whew! I've straightened one whole drawer. Time for an MTV break!").

When Certain Words Go Up or Down

Sometimes you may find in your writing one word or phrase that is either dropped or raised. Some graphologists believe that the more uphill a word is written, the more positive the writer feels about the word.

For example, notice how in this sentence the name "Zoe" goes up:

I don't know who to invite to the dance - Zoe or Janna?

This writer may be giving away the fact that he's more "up" on Zoe than he is on Janna. He'll probably end up asking her.

 # Write On! Exercise #4

Ask a few friends to think of two celebrities they like and two they don't like. Next, have them write down the following sentence four times, each time substituting one star's name for the other: "[Star's name] is totally awesome!"

After your friends are finished, compare sentences. Can you tell which stars they like best simply by looking at the baseline and seeing if the celebrity names go up or down?

This exercise works better if you use samples written on unlined paper. The baseline will be much more dramatic.

The Bottom Line

Do you prefer to write on lined or unlined paper? In general, if you only feel comfortable with lined paper, you're expressing your need for rules and regulations. You feel safer writing within a specified space, just the way you feel more comfortable in life acting within certain boundaries. For example, let's say your older brother forbids you to enter his room. He's even hung a skull and crossbones on his door to discourage you. Per Brother's orders, you stay out of the room!

On the other hand, if you prefer unlined paper, you're probably more free-thinking and spontaneous. You don't like rules, and fight against anyone trying to tell you what to do. Skull and crossbones, good luck! A moat full of piranhas wouldn't stop you from walking into that room!

laying it on thick: pen and pencil pressure

I n order to write, you must bear down on your pen or pencil with a certain amount of pressure. Graphologists believe that the amount of pressure people use indicates how much energy and enthusiasm they have in life.

Pressure also indicates how stressed out a writer is. When people are relaxed, they tend to press down on a pen or pencil gently and write relatively lightly. If they're uptight, they'll press down harder and their writing will be heavier.

The pressure of handwriting can also change due to illness. When people are sick, their writing is often fainter than when they're well because they aren't feeling as energetic as usual.

 Write On! Exercise #5

By changing the force with which you write, you can sometimes change your mood. The next time you're feeling stressed out, write this sentence: "I'm getting so relaxed, I'm about to fall asleep."

First write the sentence using very heavy pressure. Notice that writing this way makes you feel even tenser.

Then write the sentence using a very light hand. Do it again. By the second time, do you notice that you're starting to actually *feel* more relaxed? It's almost impossible to stay stressed out when you press lightly on the paper.

Various Pressure Types

Very Heavy Pressure

I'm a really heavy dude.

If you bear down this hard, you're probably totally and completely stressed out. Feeling frustrated about school? Your parents? Your friends? You may be taking it out on the page.

Keep in mind that kids age eleven to fourteen will write with heavier pressure more often than adults because their bodies are going through (or beginning to go through) many intense physical and emotional changes.

Heavy Pressure

I'm a heavy dude.

If you usually write like this, you probably want to leave your mark on the world, just as you leave a strong mark on the paper. The force of your writing says "Notice me!"

You're no doubt strong, dynamic, and determined. You may only be in the sixth grade, but if you could, you'd run for eighth-grade president. You could easily do a better job than any of those older kids.

Medium Pressure

I'm a dude.

Most people write with medium or average pressure. You may not have the energy to run a marathon, but you definitely have what it takes to keep up with other kids your age.

Light Pressure

I'm a lightweight.

If you usually have light handwriting, you're probably an easygoing, *light*hearted person. You like to relax and don't feel you always have to go, go, go. You also don't get rattled very easily, even when faced with a pop essay test on a poem you never *did* get around to reading.

Very Light Pressure

Can you even see this?

If you find yourself writing this lightly, it may be a sign you're feeling insecure. You may feel as if you want to disappear, just as your handwriting is almost doing! You probably need to spend some time pumping up your ego, reminding yourself of the things you do really well.

Uneven Pressure

My mind is somewhere else.

If you write both hard and lightly within one handwriting sample, it may mean you're distracted and worried about something. It could also signify that you're just too busy to pay attention to how evenly you put pressure on a pen!

Pressure on Certain Words or Phrases

If you put pressure on a specific word or phrase, you probably feel more positive or deeply about that word or phrase.

For example, look at the following sentence:

Over the holidays, I visited my grandparents, my uncle, my aunt, and my two cousins.

Notice how "aunt" is written much more lightly than "grandparents," "uncle," and "two cousins." This writer obviously doesn't think as much of his aunt as he does of the rest of his family. By almost "disappearing" her name, what he's really saying is "I wish *she'd* visit her other relatives over the holidays!"

Now take a look at these two writers:

Writer A:

I will always love Michael!

Writer B:

No, I will always love Michael!

Which of these two girls is more likely to date Michael for a longer time? If you picked Writer B, you're correct. The force with which she wrote this sentence reveals her "heavy," long-lasting feelings for Michael. The other writer's feelings are probably not so deep.

Write On! Exercise #6

Gather together two or three friends. Ask each one to write the following sentence: "I wonder what you're going to do with this sentence once I've written it."

Next, ask each friend how he or she is feeling. Energetic or tired? Relaxed or stressed? Then compare the pressure of each person's handwriting with his or her mood. Do they match up? Can you tell who has the least (or most) energy and who is the most (or least) relaxed by looking only at their handwriting?

Pencil or Pen ?

The pressure of a person's writing also depends on what implement the person uses. Obviously a thick, felt-tipped pen will make a heavier mark than a pencil. You'll need to first consider the type of writing instrument that was used before you analyze a handwriting sample.

zoned out:
writing zones and loops

G raphologists have divided the writing space into three zones.

Upper zone	
Middle zone	*help*
Lower zone	

Each zone reflects a different part of your personality.

The upper zone represents your thinking self—all of your thoughts and dreams. For example, are you a good student who actually enjoys going to school? Do you love to curl up with a good book and read? Do you often just sit around and daydream? The amount of time and energy you devote to thinking and dreaming shows up in your upper zone.

The middle zone stands for your social self—how you interact with other people. Do you feel most happy with the phone permanently connected to your ear while you chat with all of your friends? Do you love to rush from crowd to crowd at school, talking to as many people as humanly possible in the four and a half minutes between classes? Or are you more inclined to be on the shy side, and have a few tried-and-true best friends? Maybe your moods vary between the two? This part of your personality will be reflected in your middle zone.

The lower zone symbolizes your physical self—your health and how you feel about your body. It also represents your attitude about material possessions and money. Are you an athlete who likes nothing better than playing four hours of baseball or basketball? Are you sometimes overly concerned with your looks, obsessing about your hair or what you're wearing? Your innermost feelings about your physical self are reflected in how much you use the lower zone.

Graphologists believe that a well-balanced person will write like this:

Notice how the upper, middle, and lower zone are all the same size and shape. No one zone is emphasized. But if one of the zones dominates the other two, then it may be saying something about how you feel about yourself.

A Dominating Upper Zone

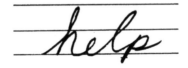

If your upper zone dominates your handwriting, you're a big thinker. You probably love school and can spend hours pondering a question like "If a tree falls in the woods and no one is nearby to hear it, does it still make a sound?" You also enjoy daydreaming about what your life will be like in five or ten years.

Sometimes, however, your thoughts may be so high in the sky that you forget about reality. You may forget to brush your teeth or do the dishes, or you may wear mismatched socks. People may tease you about having your head in the clouds.

A Dominating Middle Zone

help

If your middle zone dominates your handwriting, you're a people person. You spend most of your energy trying to get along with people and thinking about others.

Sometimes, however, you get so caught up in pleasing other people that you forget to spend a few minutes each day simply thinking about yourself and your needs. You're the type to spend Saturday morning washing the family car and Saturday afternoon tutoring a friend in math. By the end of the day, you realize that you never got around to doing any of the things *you* wanted to do, like whipping up a batch of cookies or reading the latest X-Men comic book.

A Dominating Lower Zone

help

If your lower zone dominates your handwriting, you're probably a good athlete. You're also probably very concerned about your appearance—when you're going to a party, you're apt to change clothes two or three times before settling on an outfit. People with dominant lower zones also love to collect things—CDs, computer games, books, Pogs—you name it!

37

The Lowdown on Loops

Many people tack on loops to letters that extend into the upper or lower zones. What do *they* reveal about personality?

Tall Upper Loops

If your upper loops are long, you've got big goals in life. You aren't afraid to pursue even your tallest dreams!

Full Upper Loops

The fatter your upper loops are, the more time you spend thinking. Think of each loop as a balloon waiting to be filled with thoughts. Usually, the fuller the loop, the more creative and imaginative the writer.

Pointed Upper Loops

If you're a pretty stressed-out person, you probably write this way. The more relaxed a person is, the more rounded his or her loops are.

Stick-Figure Upper Loops

If you make your loops like this, you're probably very efficient and good at avoiding needless work (such as making loops when you don't need any). You move fast and make quick, smart decisions.

Long Lower Loops

laugh

The longer your lower loops, the more restless you probably are. You're the type who starts squirming after ten minutes of class.

Fat Lower Loops

laugh

The fatter your lower loop, the more you want out of life. Think of each loop as a sack waiting to be filled up—with love, money, or the roar of a cheering crowd!

Write On! Exercise #7

Are you dominated by your upper, middle, or lower zone, or are you perfectly balanced among the three? Using lined paper, write the following words:

leggy	handwriting
walking	perfect
enjoyable	helpful
fabulous	yell

Look back over this chapter and re-read pages 35–37. Does your handwriting reveal that you're more of a thinker, a social animal, or an athlete? Do you agree with what your handwriting is saying?

What a Bod!

To remember what each of the three zones symbolizes, compare the zones to the human body.

The upper zone is the head, where all our thinking takes place.

The middle zone corresponds to the parts of our bodies that we use to socialize (like, for example, our hands, which we use to greet people with).

The lower zone corresponds to our body as well as our attachment to "earthly" possessions.

different strokes for different folks: connecting and final strokes

Connecting strokes are what join letters together in cursive handwriting. Final strokes are the strokes at the end of each word.

Connecting Strokes

There are four types of connecting strokes: garlands, arcades, angles, and threads. Most people usually write with one type of connecting stroke.

Garlands

A garland connects letters with an underhand stroke. To best understand what a garland is, trace the word above with your finger. Notice how you connect the letters by going underneath them.

If you write mainly with garlands, chances are you're open, warm, and giving. Notice how even the shape of the garland looks open and inviting, like an upturned palm. You're easy to get along with and hardly ever get into fights with your parents or friends.

Arcades

when

An arcade connects letters with an overhand stroke. Trace the word above with your finger to best understand what an arcade is. See how you connect the letters by going over them. They almost form a protective shelter over the words.

If you write mainly with arcades, you're probably very protective of your family, friends, and companion animals. You look out for those you love and expect them to look out for you.

In general, people who write with arcades are more controlled than garland writers. It takes more thought to write arcades, which means that you probably spend more time planning your actions than the impulsive garland writer. For example, you'd probably never dash off a love letter to your latest crush and drop it in the mail. You'd re-read and revise it at least twenty times, then probably just stuff it in a drawer.

Angles

when

An angle connects letters with sharply angled strokes, forming a "V."

If you write mainly with connecting angles, you may be as "sharp" as an angle! You're probably smart, aggressive, hardworking, competitive, and at times, pretty stressed out. When people are relaxed, they tend to round out their writing. When they're feeling uptight, their writing gets more pointy.

When

A thread connects letters with a squiggly line. Sometimes the line is so squiggly, it almost makes the letters unreadable.

If you write mainly with threads, you're probably in a constant rush. You don't have time to spend ten minutes writing out a phone message for your mom. You've got soccer practice, then band rehearsal, then an extra-credit paper to write! Instead of writing using strong connecting strokes, you hurry and string together the letters with as little work as possible—a mere thread.

Connecting letters with threads may also mean that you're the type to have ten things on your mind at once. You're too busy thinking about the big party you're planning and what's happening on *Beavis and Butt-head* to pay too much attention to how you connect your letters.

Final Strokes

Final strokes are the little extra strokes people use to finish off a word. Let's look at a few different types and what they may mean:

☞ If your final strokes are short, you probably know what you want in life and have no trouble making decisions.

☞ Long final strokes mean you're very giving and generous.

☞ If your final strokes underscore words, you're independent. The line says: "I can stand all by myself, thank you very much!"

☞ If your final strokes are high and curl over the last letter, you enjoy a lot of attention. This extra stroke screams: "Notice me!"

☞ Final strokes that turn downward mean that you're probably feeling down as well.

☞ If your final strokes stretch to the right, you're probably very goal-oriented.

☞ If your final strokes go backward, you may be very attached to the past.

First Impressions on Initial Strokes

When people first learn to write, they often start words with an initial stroke as an extra flourish. However, as people become more at ease with writing, they usually drop initial strokes for speed's sake. They simply take too much extra time! So, if you are analyzing someone's handwriting and the beginnings of words have initial strokes, this person is most likely just learning to write.

 ## Write On! Exercise #8

Grab a few friends or family members and ask them to write the following sentence: "Different strokes for different folks." Judging solely by their connecting strokes, and whether each uses mainly garlands, arcades, angles, or threads, can you tell who is more impulsive, who is more social, who is the most competitive, and who is always in a hurry? The connecting strokes should give you good clues. Afterward, compare what the handwriting reveals with what you already know about the people.

dot your "i's" and cross your "t's"

Graphologists spend more time studying some letters than others. The small "i" and "t" are two of the most important letters in handwriting analysis. The "i" dots and "t" bars (the horizontal line crossing the stem of the "t") reveal volumes about one's personality.

Why? Each "i" you dot and "t" you cross requires a little extra thought. There are dozens of ways you could do either. How you choose reflects your personality.

The "i's" Have It!

A Dot Placed Precisely Over the "i"

You're a stickler for accuracy! You like to get things done just right. You're so neat you probably alphabetize your CD collection and organize your clothing closet by color.

A Dot "Flung" High Above the "i"

You're a go-getter with a lot of imagination. You may also be a bit of a daydreamer with big goals for the future: the first MTV videojock to become President of the United States, perhaps?

A Thick Dot

This may mean either of two *very* *different* things. You may be feeling super-confident, the dot being a symbol of this confidence. Or the heavy dot may show that you're feeling weighted down by something. Maybe you're under a lot of pressure, or you've got an unusual amount of responsibility on your shoulders (like your mom just returned to the work force and you've become the designated short-order cook five nights a week!).

A Dot That Forms a Circle or a Heart

If you draw a circle over each "i," you're an original. You want to be noticed—and probably always are! You're the type to be the first in your crowd to flaunt a new fashion or trend, and the first to get bored with it as well.

If you like to dot your "i" with a heart, you're not only very creative, you're a true romantic.

A Dot That Slants Downward

You're probably stubborn. You've got strong opinions, and you're not afraid to share them with others.

A Dot That Looks Like an Arc

No doubt you have a great sense of humor. (Notice how the arc looks like a smiling mouth.) You love to laugh and don't take the little everyday problems in life seriously.

A Dot to the Right of the "i"

You have a tendency to act before you think and to rush through life. The "i" dot, like a lot of your ideas, is an afterthought!

A Dot to the Left of the "i"

You may be feeling down or very cautious about life. Something or someone may be holding you back from getting what you want out of life (like, how can you grow up to be a famous drummer when your parents won't allow a drum set in the house?).

No Dots

You have a tendency to be a tad forgetful and careless. (This may also mean you were simply in a hurry to finish what you were writing!)

Inconsistent Dots

If you dot your "i's" several different ways, chances are you're versatile and changeable—simply too unpredictable to dot your "i" the same way twice!

"t" Bar Personality Traits

Just as you may dot your "i's" in various ways, you may also cross your "t's" differently—even within one piece of writing! (This means, by the way, that you enjoy change and variety.) Find the most common way you cross your "t's," then analyze what it means.

A Perfectly Straight "t" Bar

You're probably a perfectionist and very self-disciplined to boot (i.e., the only one in your family who can resist Mom's homemade thousand-

47

calorie-a-pop brownies).

A Floating "t" Bar

You're ambitious and reach for the stars. Some
of your ideas may be a little impractical, but
you never lose your enthusiasm!

A Slanted "t" Bar

If your "t" bar slants downward, you're apt
to be very stubborn. When you want something, nothing can stand in your way.

If your "t" bar slants upward, you're
probably a dreamer, full of imagination.

A Right-Sided "t" Bar

You're probably pretty impatient. You hate
to sit in one place—even in a movie theater
watching the latest Keanu Reeves flick—for too long. You
almost always think and move quickly. While you get a lot
done, sometimes you sacrifice quality for quantity.

A Left-Sided "t" Bar

Most likely, you're a procrastinator. You just
can't seem to return those darn videos on
time, and your philosophy probably is, Why read a chapter
of geology homework now when I can read it tomorrow?

A Long "t" Bar

You're confident and not afraid to take
chances or be noticed—such as the time you
went to school dressed up like an elf for St. Patrick's Day!

A Knotted "t" Bar

You're probably very persistent and stubborn. Once you grab hold of an idea or project, you won't let go.

A Curved "t" Bar

If your "t" bar curves into slight curlicues (in any direction) on each end, you're a true romantic. You hate to admit it, but some sappy TV commercials bring tears to your eyes.

If your "t" bar curves downward in an arc, you enjoy being in control. Sometimes, however, this may get in the way of being as wild and crazy as you'd like.

If your curved "t" bar soars upward, you're easygoing. You'd rather get along with everyone than make waves.

A Double-Crossed "t" Bar

You're very efficient! Why waste time crossing two "t's" when you can save precious moments and cross them both at once? This is the exact same way you approach life.

letter

No "t" Bar

If you don't cross your "t's" at all, it can mean that you're careless, forgetful, or in a big hurry. It may also mean that you hate to hassle with little details in life.

Different "t" Bars

If you cross your "t's" differently in the same sample, you like change. You're the type who makes it a personal goal to taste every single flavor available at your local ice cream parlor.

Making a Connection

Most people cross their "t's" the same way they dot their "i's." For example, if you dot your "i's" perfectly, you probably cross your "t's" perfectly, too.

When you study these two letters together, you get a double-whammy insight into a writer's personality.

A Cast of Hundreds

Because there are literally hundreds of ways to dot an "i" or cross a "t," you may not be able to find your exact method described in this chapter. When analyzing a "t" bar or "i" dot *not* mentioned, take what you do know about "t's" and "i's" and apply those *general* ideas to the handwriting. Most likely, you'll come up with a pretty accurate interpretation.

Write On! Exercise #9

Ask your friends to write down the following words that contain "i's" and "t's":

graffiti

little

icicle

think

indicate

third

indigestion

time-out

industry

title

infant

(Don't tell them why. They may get self-conscious and not dot their "i's" or cross their "t's" the way they normally do.)

Grab a sheet of paper and write these words yourself. Find the type of "i" dot and "t" bar that is done most often within each sample. What do the dots and bars say about you and your friends? (Take special note of any similarities between an individual's "i" dots and "t" bars!)

let's get personal: the pronoun "I"

Every time you write the personal pronoun "I," you give away how you feel about yourself. The "I" represents your self-image, how you see yourself in relation to the world. Perhaps no other letter tells so much about you!

For example, which of the following three people thinks the most about himself?

Person A:

I can't think of anyone I'd rather be than me!

Person B:

I can't think of anyone I'd rather be than me!

Person C:

I can't think of anyone I'd rather be than me!

If you guessed Person B, you're right. The "I" is big and fancy, complete with loops. The size and attention paid to writing the "I" says that the author thinks he or she is very important.

Large "I"

I like myself.

If your "I" is oversize, you're probably very self-confident. Maybe a little *too* confident sometimes.

Small "I"

I like myself – sometimes!

If your "I" is small, you may feel a little underconfident. You're blind to all your wonderful traits and talents!

Average "I"

I'm pretty darn balanced.

If your "I" looks like this, you're self-assured and confident without being cocky.

Elaborate "I"

I love me!

If you've got the fanciest "I" on the block, it may be because you crave attention. You want to be noticed—and your "I" certainly is!

Lower-Case "I"

i need confidence.

If you make your "I" an "i," it may mean you don't have as much self-esteem as you should. At times, you probably don't feel very good about yourself.

Printed "I" with Serifs

I can do it!

If you print your "I," you likely include two small lines drawn in above and below the "I" stem. These are called serifs. If you favor this type of "I," you're probably very independent. These two extra lines connected to the "I" stem emphasize the fact that you can rely on yourself and don't need a lot of help from other people.

Left-Leaning "I"

I'm doing okay.

If your "I" leans to the left, you're probably on the shy side. Also, since any back-slanted handwriting may reveal a negative feeling, this type of "I" may show that you don't think very highly of yourself.

Right-Leaning "I"

I love people.

If your "I" leans to the right, you're a people person. The slant to the right may also indicate that you feel great about yourself.

An "I" with a Hook

I wanna be a kid forever!

I wanna grow up!

Hooks, in general, signify people's desire to hang on to something. Remember how graphologists believe that the left-hand side of the page refers to the past and the right-hand side of the page to the future? If your "I" hooks to the left, you may be hung up on the past. If your "I" hooks to the right, you're more interested in where you're going than where you've been.

 Write On! Exercise #10

Who has the biggest ego in your family? Who's the most creative? Ask everyone in your family to write down the following sentence: "I know what I want and I get it."

This gives you three "I's" to play with from each person. Using the information you just learned, see what new insights you can find into your family.

When the Pronoun "I" Is Slanted Differently

Look at this sentence:

$\mathcal{I}$ can't believe what happened to Tiffany.

   Notice that the "I" is slanted to the left while the rest of the sentence is slanted to the right. What does this say about the writer?
   Well, according to Andrea McNichol's book, *Handwriting Analysis: Putting It to Work for You,* 35 percent of American adults slant the pronoun "I" to the left, or write it straight up and down, when the rest of their handwriting slants to the right. This can mean, says McNichol, that a writer feels insecure or hesitant about expressing himself or herself. People who slant their "I's" this way are happy talking about *other* people, but aren't eager to reveal how *they* are feeling themselves.
   This writer may feel comfortable discussing Tiffany's tragedy, but probably won't open up about her own troubles.

what's in a name: the significance of signatures

Your handwriting reveals the real you, the inner you. Your signature, however, reveals the public you, how you want others to see you. That's why a person's handwriting is often different from his or her signature.

Think about it. If you're like most kids, you've probably spent hours playing around with your signature. You practice writing it this way and that, dreaming about the day when you're famous and crowds of adoring fans beg for your autograph!

How your signature varies from the rest of your writing can tell a lot about you. You can even discover things about yourself by just looking at your signature alone.

A Signature Larger Than the Other Writing

Jody,
Want to go out
for lunch?

Amy

You act very confident around others—more self-confident than you probably feel! In fact, you may be using a large signature as a way to make up for feeling insecure.

A Signature Smaller Than the Other Writing

Grandma,
I made the
volleyball team!
Janet

You're the modest type. You may be loaded with talent and ability, but you don't want to shout it to the world. You're the type who, after receiving a perfect report card, shrugs your shoulders and says, "I was just lucky."

A Signature the Same Size as the Other Writing

Mom,
Went to the store.
Kate

What you see is what you get. You're the same on the inside as you are on the outside. You're honest, don't like games, and wish other people didn't either!

An Unclear Signature

If your signature is barely legible, it may be a sign that you don't want others to know who you are. You feel that, some-

how, your unreadable scrawl is
actually protecting you from other
people. No doubt you only let
down your guard around family
and best friends. Or your scrawl
may mean that you're simply in a
hurry and don't have much time
to sign your name.

A Signature with Overly Large Capital Letters

This is a sign that you dream of
being famous. Those extra-big
capital letters scream: "I want to
stand out and be noticed!"
You've probably already begun
planning your Academy Award
acceptance speech.

An Underlined Signature

If you underline your name with just one line, it's a sign that
you're confident and self-assured. However, if you add too
many lines or flourishes, it may mean you're actually feeling
insecure. You're using the extra flash and dash to make up
for feeling not very noticeable inside!

An Overscored Signature

See how the line above the signature provides a sort of "shelter" for the signature, a roof of sorts. This may mean you want to be protected from the world. It's your way of defending yourself.

A Signature with a Line Through It

Notice how this line "destroys" the name. This may mean that you'd like to get rid of your image and find a whole new one! For example, maybe you're tired of being labeled class egghead and wish for once you could be thought of as class Deadhead.

An Artsy Signature

In general, the more creative your signature, the more creative a person you are—and the more you want others to know it! A creative signature may also be a sign that you want to draw a lot of attention to yourself, just as your signature is an attention-getter.

Write On! Exercise #11

What do the signatures of your favorite celebrities tell you?
(Maybe more than you'll discover watching them act or
sing!) Here are the signatures of some of today's hottest
stars. Can you tell which one is really shy and insecure?
Which one obviously dreams of becoming famous? Which
one seems to have a creative personality? Which appears
comfortable with himself or herself? And, most important,
which star might you be most compatible with? Once you've
studied their signatures, you may never look at your favorite
celebrities the same way again!

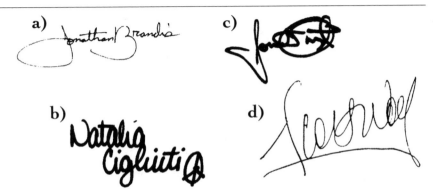

a) With his extra-big initial letters, Jonathan Brandis, star
of *seaQuest,* seems to have *extra-big* dreams of being famous.
b) Lindsay in *Saved by the Bell: The New Class,* actress Natalia
Cigliuti certainly has a creative flair. See her peace sign and
fun initial letters?
c) Who is this celebrity who seems to want to hide behind
his unreadable signature? Jonathan Angel from *Saved by the
Bell: The New Class.* Then again, he may have just been in a
hurry to get to his next scene!
d) With the single underline emphasizing his signature,
Scott Wolf from *Party of Five* appears confident and comfortable with himself.

spaced out! the space between words, letters, and lines

When you write, you naturally leave a certain amount of space between letters and words, as well as between different lines of writing. Some people squash their letters, words, and lines close together; others leave lots of room in between. Graphologists believe that these spaces reveal a lot about how people interact with others and how they feel about themselves.

Word Spacing

Many handwriting analysts believe that how much space you leave between words reflects how you act around other people. If you put a lot of space between words, you probably put a lot of distance between you and the people in your life. If you write your words very close together, you probably prefer close contact with your friends and family.

Narrow Word Spacing

I bet you can't tell when one word starts and one word ends.

If you write your words this close together, you most likely love being with other people. You're happiest when surrounded by twenty friends—and talking to ten of them at once! While you're probably popular and liked by everyone, you also have a tendency to be disorganized. Your life is filled with so many people, it may become as cluttered as your handwriting appears.

Average Word Spacing

This writing looks normal to me.

This type of spacing shows a person who's balanced when it comes to spending time with friends and time alone. You enjoy being with others, but also like some time to yourself.

Wide Word Spacing

Do these words seem too far apart?

If you put a lot of space in between each word you write, you're probably a more private person. You keep your feelings inside and open up only to a few trusted pals.

Letter Spacing

Graphologists believe that the space between letters reveals how relaxed you are and how open you are to new situations and ideas.

Narrow Spaces Between Letters

These letters can't breathe!

How do you feel just looking at these cramped letters? Closed in? A little uptight? If you write this way, you may be feeling trapped in a certain situation, or you may not be able to see beyond your own point of view. For instance, maybe just as you get settled in school and begin to make some close friends, your parents decide to move across the country. What can you do? You may feel completely stuck, because you can't exactly rent your own apartment. Your frustration will be apparent in your writing.

Average Spaces Between Letters

I am so normal.

Overall, you're a fairly relaxed person. Sure, you may feel stressed now and then, but who doesn't? In general, you try to understand other people's points of view, even if you don't always agree with them—such as the time you kept an open mind about your sister when she decided to pierce her eyebrow!

Wide Spaces Between Letters

These letters have lots of room.

In general, if you put wide spaces between your letters, you're so relaxed that nothing much bothers you. You can be so open to new ideas that sometimes you get involved in projects and situations before having thoroughly checked them out. It wouldn't be out of character for you to impulsively sign up for drama club, only to remember later that you have such terrible stage fright you'd probably drop dead if you ever had to actually perform!

Some graphologists also believe that wide spaces between letters are a sign of generosity. For instance, you're probably the type who, if a friend mentions she likes your new ankle chain, will give it to her.

Line Spacing

The amount of space you leave between lines is an indication of how in control you are of your life.

When Lines Are Too Close Together

I'm starting to feel all tangled up!

If you write with tangled lines, as shown above, it may mean you're feeling overwhelmed by life. You're probably wrestling with some confusing issues, such as how come all your friends are becoming interested in the opposite sex when you couldn't care less.

When Lines Are Average-Spaced

Is there such a thing as too normal?

You're feeling in control. And while your life isn't completely organized (you've returned your share of overdue books to the library), you've basically got a good handle on school, friends, and family.

When Lines Are Too Far Apart

Like my food, I don't like my lines to touch either.

Interestingly, this can mean the exact same thing as when a writer's lines are too close together. When lines are this far apart, you may be feeling confused or "spacey." (As in, How can any normal twelve-year-old be expected to read and understand two chapters on plant reproduction in one night?)

 ## Write On! Exercise #12

The amount of space between your letters can indicate how hassled you are feeling. The closer the letters, the more uptight the writer is. Test this out for yourself by asking a friend first to relax for a minute (he or she can do this by sitting quietly and taking deep breaths), and then to write the following sentences: "I've never really thought about how much space I put between my letters. I wonder just how spacey I really am."

Next, ask your friend to think about something that really stresses him or her out—like giving a speech in class or running a mile in gym. Then have your friend write the sentences again.

Compare samples to see if the spacing between the letters is different when your friend feels relaxed than when he or she is feeling stressed.

How to Tell (Most of the Time!) if Someone Is Lying

$\int$ ome graphologists believe that if there is a space before a certain word, it indicates that the writer is lying. For instance, check out the following sentence:

I can't wait to come to your house. Now that I'm 13, do you think I can play football with you and your friends?

This is part of a letter written by a young boy to his fifteen-year-old cousin, who had invited him over for a weekend visit. Take a closer look at the sentence. Notice how there is some extra space before the "13." Why did the boy put extra space there? Because he's lying. He's really only ten, but he's hoping his cousin forgot how old he is. The younger boy thinks that if he tells his cousin he's thirteen, the older boy will let him play football (tackle, of course) with him and his friends. The space reveals that he paused mentally before filling in his age.

When people have to think before they write, they may not be telling the truth. The telltale sign is the extra space!

making boundaries: margins

Graphologists, in general, believe that margins, the blank spaces bordering the written area on a page, represent walls people put up around themselves. The wider the wall—or margin—the more a person isolates himself or herself from others and from life in general.

Margins, graphologists also believe, reveal walls people put up to block out either the past or the future. Analysts make this kind of determination by examining if one margin is wider or more narrow than another.

Graphologists believe that the top of the page, as well as the left-hand side, represents the past, because as we write, moving from top to bottom and from left to right, the top and the left-hand side of the paper contain "older" words. The bottom of the page, as well as the right-hand side, contains "newer" words, representing the future. How much space or margin a writer leaves at the top, bottom, left, or right-hand side of a page, therefore, reflects his or her feelings about the past and the future.

Types of Margins

No Margin

If you fill up an entire page without leaving any margins, you probably live life to the fullest. You're likely to participate in many activities, from gardening to glee club to synchronized swimming. You also like to meet, and befriend, as many people as possible.

Four Narrow Margins

Chances are you're very outgoing and involved in many different activities, although you're probably not as extroverted as someone who writes without any margins at all. You set reasonable limits on yourself and know when you're simply too tired or too busy to pick up yet another new friend or hobby.

Four Wide Margins

If you write with wide margins, you're probably cautious in life. You tend to commit yourself to a few select activities and people. You protect yourself from getting involved in too many things, just as your handwriting is protected by a safety layer of space on each side.

Normal Margins (Four Even Margins)

For starters, you're probably neat and organized. You're also pretty conventional—no way do you wear a ring in your navel! You progress calmly and steadily through life, and you have plenty of mental space to tackle all the challenges thrown your way.

Wide Left Margin

Because the left-hand side of the page represents the past, if you write with a wide left margin, it can mean you're trying to distance yourself from the past. For example, maybe you're trying to forget something painful—your parents' divorce, a breakup with a friend you've grown apart from. You're ready to move on and can't wait for all the good things the future will bring!

THE SPRING MUSICAL IS IN TWO WEEKS AND I HAVE THE LEAD. I'M SO EXCITED! AND THEN AFTER THAT, SCHOOL'S OUT AND MY FAMILY AND I ARE DRIVING TO CHICAGO TO SEE MY AUNT AND UNCLE, THEN, I START TRAINING FOR VOLLEYBALL. I MAY EVEN TRY OUT FOR CAPTAIN THIS YEAR!

Wide Right Margin

The right-hand side of the page represents the future. If your margin stops short of the right side of the page, it may mean you're distancing yourself from the future. Maybe you're a little nervous about making the jump from elementary school to junior high and instead wish things would stay the way they are.

IT'S HARD TO MOVE FORWARD, WHEN MY LIFE WAS SO SIMPLE AND COMFORTABLE IN ELEMENTARY SCHOOL, TO JUNIOR HIGH. I HOPE I CAN ADJUST AND MEET NEW FRIENDS. I JUST FEEL A LITTLE BIT UNCOMFORTABLE.

A Wide or Narrow Top Margin

Graphologists believe that people leave a wider margin at the top of the page when they're writing to someone they respect or fear. The writer feels lower and less worthy than the person, so they unconsciously "lower" themselves down on the page.

For example, if you're writing to a teacher, you might leave a big margin at the top of the page. However, if you're writing to a pal whom you feel completely at ease with, you might start in at the very top of the page.

A wide or narrow top margin may also reflect your feelings toward the past, which the top of the page represents. A wide top margin may mean you're trying to get away from something in the past. A narrow top margin may mean you're very attached to the past.

A Wide or Narrow Bottom Margin

Because the bottom of the page represents the future, if you stop short of the bottom of the page, this may be a sign you're scared to grow up and pursue your goals.

If the margin is narrow, you may love to rush headlong into new projects and plans. Whatever the future has in store, you're ready for it!

 Write On! Exercise #13

Ask a parent or friend to write a note to an authority figure in his or her life, such as a boss or teacher. Then study the letter to see where on the page it began. Next, ask the same person to write a note to a friend. Study this note to see if the writer started it at a different place on the page.

You can also tell a lot about people by the way they treat pre-existing margins, like those on most lined school notebook paper.

For example, let's say you have two best friends. One is a rebel—she has three holes in her left ear, four in her right, and a butterfly tattoo on her shoulder. The other is a quiet, computer-loving bookworm. He's a good student who prides himself on how well he gets along with his teachers.

When writing on lined paper with built-in margins, which one of your friends do you think would tend to ignore the margins?

If you guessed your rebel friend, you're right. Now think again. What if your one-of-a-kind, crazy friend kept perfect margins, while your quiet, responsible buddy wrote all over the place, ignoring every margin? This could uncover some hidden personality trait about your friends that you never knew!

People's use of margins says volumes about how adventuresome they are, and how likely they are to break the rules—regardless of their appearance.

give yourself a hand: putting it all together

By now, you're probably itching to get your hands on a handwriting sample and use all that you've learned to come up with your very first complete handwriting analysis.

The first thing to do is to obtain a handwriting sample from the person you want to analyze. Make sure the sample is at least several sentences long so you can get a good enough feel for how that person writes. If possible, get a sample written on unlined paper without built-in margins, so you can better analyze the writer's baseline and use of margins.

Now go through the handwriting sample, analyzing it element by element. Use the following checklist so you don't forget anything.

1. What is the slant of the handwriting?

Does it slant to the right? The left? Straight up and down? In all directions?

2. What is the size of the handwriting?

Does it vary? Are certain words or phrases bigger or smaller than others?

3. Which way does the baseline go?

Does the writing slope up, slope down, run straight across, or slope both up and down?

4. How heavily is the writer bearing down on the paper?

Is the pressure heavy? Very heavy? Light? Super-light? Average?

5. Which zone dominates the handwriting?

The upper, middle, or lower? Or are all three balanced?

6. What type of strokes is used between the letters?

Does the writer use mainly garlands, arcades, angles, or threads?

7. How are the "i's" dotted and the "t's" crossed?

Are the "i's" dotted consistently, or are they all over the place? Does the "t" bar cross the "t" stem in the same place for every "t"? Does it vary?

8. How is the pronoun "I" written?

Is it oversize, undersize, or simple?

9. What does the signature look like?

Is any part of the signature larger or smaller than the others? Does the signature look different from the rest of the handwriting? If so, how?

10. How much space is there between words, letters, and lines?

Are words and letters spaced closely together, making it difficult to read? Do lines get tangled because they're so close to each other?

11. What are the margins of the paper?

Are they even? Bigger on the left? On the right? Smaller on the top? On the bottom?

As a warmup, first analyze the handwriting sample on page 4. Write down each observation on a piece of paper. Together, they should add up to a pretty complete picture of what sort of person I (Alison Bell) am. Do your observations match up with my self-analysis below?

1. My handwriting slants a bit to the right, so I'm pretty excited about the future, especially when it comes to what I'm eating for dessert!

2. The size of my handwriting is average, meaning that I'm comfortable with myself.

3. The baseline runs slightly upward, which says I'm pretty optimistic about life and I'm not afraid to reach for my goals.

4. I bear down on my pen with lighter pressure, which means that I'm easygoing. I definitely enjoy my time to relax!

5. My handwriting is dominated by the lower zone, and my lower loops are huge! This means that I want a lot out of life, especially nice things, like clothes, a decent car, and a great stereo system.

6. I use mainly garlands to connect my letters, proving how open and giving I am!

7. I don't dot my "i's," which shows that I have a tendency to be forgetful. Also, my "t's" are crossed with an upward-curved "t" bar, showing that I like to get along with people rather than make waves.

8. I definitely write the pronoun "I" differently from the rest of my writing. I give it a big loop at the top — I LOVE TO BE NOTICED!

9. My signature is slightly larger than the rest of the words I've written. This probably means that sometimes I act more confident around people than I actually feel.

10. There is very little space between my lines — my words are constantly getting tangled. This means that at times I get overwhelmed with life — especially when I have three new books to write, which are all due to their publishers on the same day! My words and letters are average-spaced, showing that I like to spend time with my friends as well as time alone.

11. While it's hard to tell on this sample, I have a larger left margin and a narrower right margin. This shows that I'm not so eager to delve into my past, but I can't wait to see what the future brings!

Get the idea?

Once you've analyzed one sample from someone, ask him or her for a couple more to study as well. Because people's handwriting can sometimes fluctuate from day to day, this will help give you the most accurate reading of a person's *true* handwriting.

When you're finished, share your insights with the other person. Get a reaction to see how "write on" he or she thinks your analysis is.

The more handwriting samples you study, the better you'll become at graphology. And the better you become, the more you'll continue to enjoy this astonishing skill for the rest of your life!

So You Want to Know More About Handwriting Analysis?

If you are interested in learning more about the science of graphology, here are several books (all found in the adult nonfiction section) you might enjoy:

You Are What You Write, by Huntington Hartford, published by Macmillan Publishing Company, New York, 1973.

Handwriting & Personality: How Graphology Reveals What Makes People Tick, by Ann Mahony, published by Ivy Books, New York, 1989.

Instant People: Reading Through Handwriting, by Anne Conway, published by Sterling Publishing Company, New York, 1989.

Handwriting Analysis: Putting It to Work for You, by Andrea McNichol, published by Contemporary Books, Chicago, 1991.

Interpreting Handwriting, by Jane Paterson, published by David McKay Company, New York, 1976.

Handwriting as a Key to Personality, by Klara Romans, published by Pantheon Books, New York, 1952.

For more information, you can also write to:

Nancy Kowalski, librarian
The American Association of Handwriting Analysts
420 Rogers St.
Downers Grove, IL 60515